Workbook for Jay Shetty's
8 Rules of Love

Printed Exercises for Reflection, Processing, and Practising the Lessons

 BIG ACTION BOOKS

BigActionBooks.com

Contents

Introduction

Don't just <u>read about</u> how to find love, keep it and let it go; actually <u>practice it</u>.

WHY THIS WORKBOOK?
You've read Jay Shetty's fabulous book about how to find love, keep it, and let it go. Now it's time to actually *practice* it - write; journal; put the lessons in motion.

This workbook was created as a **companion** to Jay Shetty's "8 Rules of Love". While reading the book, we found ourselves wishing for a place where we could write, process and practise the book's exercises in a constructive, concise way. The exercises are excellent - but there isn't much space to actually write in the book itself. Instead, we found ourselves cobbling them together in various places - notebooks, journals, pieces of paper - all of which would eventually get lost, or at the very least, not be helpful in putting the lessons into practice. That's how this workbook was born.

HOW TO USE THIS WORKBOOK
This workbook is like a faithful friend to 8 Rules of Love. In it, you'll find exactly what's advertised: the exercises from the book, summarised and formatted, with space to answer.

- All exercises from 8 Rules of Love, extracted into one single place
- Space to write under each exercise
- Lists, ruled lines and space for you to answer, journal and reflect
- Clearly organised and well-formatted so it's easy to follow

In each section, we've extracted the main premise of the exercise, and then added space to respond and practise the lessons. This may come in the format of a table to fill in, space to free-write, or other exercise methods to provide space for reflection. You'll also notice the "Parts" and "Chapters" referenced in the book, so you can easily find the section if you need to look back on it for further context.

If you want to not only read about how to find, keep and let go of love - but also put the lessons into practice - this workbook, as well as your own dedication, will help you do just that.

Enjoy, and thank you.
Let's dive in!

---

* Please note: This is an unofficial workbook companion for 8 Rules of Love to help motivated do-ers process the lessons from this fantastic book. It is not created by or associated with Jay Shetty in any official way.

Part One: Solitude: Learning to Love Yourself

RULE 1: LET YOURSELF BE ALONE

TRY THIS: Solo Audit

1. To start off, dedicate a week to monitoring how much time you spend by yourself. This means being without a companion. Avoid aimlessly flipping through your phone or having the TV on in the background. Your objective is to keep track of active individual activities -- like reading, strolling, practicing meditation, working out, or engaging in hobbies such as cooking, visiting museums, or creating something. It's important to note that sleeping time should not be included. During this phase of the exercise, there's no need to deliberately seek solitude. Our aim is simply to observe your current habits.

After recording the time spent by yourself, jot down your activities and reflect on whether performing them without a companion affected you in any way. It's possible that you find pleasure in doing dishes alone, or perhaps it serves as a poignant reminder that you cooked for yourself. Walking alone might be enjoyable for you, or it could evoke feelings of loneliness. Take a moment to contemplate why you felt comfortable or uncomfortable in those situations. Identify the moments when you feel at ease being alone. The purpose of this exercise is to assess how you currently use your solitary time, before we proceed with cultivating your ability to be alone.

Time	Activity	Comfortable / Uncomfortable	Why?

2. Now that you've evaluated your initial level of alone time, begin incorporating a fresh solo activity into your weekly routine. The key is to intentionally select how you spend that time. Opt for an activity that you seldom or have never experienced on your own before.

- Catch a film, show, or sporting event
- Visit an art gallery
- Book a solo dinner reservation
- Dine out at a restaurant without phone distractions
- Embark on a hiking adventure
- Celebrate your birthday
- Indulge in a significant holiday
- Attend a party solo
- Participate in a unique volunteering experience
- Enroll in a MasterClass

Give this a shot on a weekly basis over the course of the upcoming month. While engaged in the activity, be mindful of your response to unfamiliar circumstances. Take note of any intrusive thoughts that hinder your ability to be by yourself. Use the following questions to contemplate and ponder upon your experience.

What's the timeframe for reaching a state of ease and comfort?

_____

_____

What kind of difference would you experience if you were in the company of someone else?

_____

_____

Do you find it easier to have a good time when you're by yourself?

_____

_____

Do you ever feel like it would be nice to have someone else around?

_____

Do you find it challenging to figure out what to do with your time?

_____

_____

Do you find that a companion's response can sway your opinion of the activity?

_____

_____

(Considering the nature of the activity), do you feel inclined to divert your attention or occupy your mind with your phone, the television, or podcasts?

_____

_____

What aspects of the experience bring you joy?

_____

_____

What are the advantages and disadvantages of being alone?

_____

_____

If going out for dinner alone makes you uneasy, what could you do to make it more comfortable? You might discover that bringing a book or some work with you helps you feel engaged and productive. Engaging in a brief and friendly conversation with the waiter could be enough to start your solo dinner experience on a positive note.

If you watch a movie by yourself and miss sharing the experience with someone, try finding a new way to express your thoughts. Write a blog post, an online review, or a journal entry about the film. The same applies to taking a class. Did you learn anything from it? What aspects did you enjoy? What would you have done differently? Consider recording a voice note where you express how you felt about the experience. While it's nice to discuss and exchange opinions with others about movies, classes, or lectures, attending them alone allows you to develop your own ideas and opinions without being influenced by someone else's preferences.

If you're not accustomed to hiking alone, set a fun and relaxed objective for yourself. It could be a physical goal, such as achieving your best time on the hike, or it could be finding something interesting to bring back with you. For example, you might embark on the hike with the aim of capturing a photo you genuinely love (which you can keep for yourself or share on social media).

The purpose of this personal exploration is to become more at ease in your own company. You're getting to know your preferences without relying on someone else's priorities and objectives. You're learning how to engage in a conversation with yourself.

TRY THIS: Get To Know Your Values

Take a moment to examine the decisions you make in various aspects of your life. Are they aligned with your values, or are they ingrained habits that you might want to alter? Below are choices to help you articulate your stance towards each aspect. However, if none of them resonate with you, feel free to jot down your own descriptions. The better you understand yourself, the more you can refine the aspects you appreciate and enhance the areas where you seek change.

TIME CHOICES	How You Describe Yourself
Social Media	a. I enjoy recording snippets of my life for my friends. b. Social media isn't my cup of tea; I prefer to live in the present moment. c. Others (specify):
Weekends/Travel	a. I'm eager to explore the world. b. Whenever I have spare time, all I crave is some relaxation. c. Others (specify):
Date night	a. I enjoy being at home and preparing meals. b. I love going out for an evening in the city. c. Others (specify):
TV	a. I watch something on the screen every evening. b. I meticulously select and stick to my preferred shows only. c. Others (specify):
Punctuality	a. I'm consistently punctual. b. I frequently arrive late. c. Others (specify):
Planning	a. I maintain a calendar and adhere to my schedule. b. I'm not fond of being bound by obligations. c. Others (specify):

HABITS	How You Describe Yourself
Organization	a. I manage to keep everything neat and tidy, ensuring bills are promptly paid. b. I want to be more on top of things and organized than my current state. c. Others (specify):
Exercise	a. I enjoy being on the move or engaging in activities for the sake of well-being. b. I struggle with finding the drive or inspiration. c. Others (specify):
Food	a. I try to maintain a healthy diet, or at least make an effort to do so. b. Life is brief—I indulge in food that pleases my taste buds. c. Others (specify):
Sleep	a. If circumstances allow, I enjoy sleeping in. b. I tend to wake up early. c. Others (specify):

MONEY	How You Describe Yourself
Discretionary spending	a. My main priority is setting aside funds for the future. b. I utilize my money once I have it available. c. Others (specify):
Vacations	a. I love going on lavish vacations b. I go on trips while being mindful of my expenses c. Others (specify):
Home, clothing, car	a. I prefer to keep things straightforward. b. I enjoy indulging in the more exquisite pleasures. c. Others (specify):
Purchases	a. I make impulsive purchases b. I thoroughly think through my buying decisions c. Others (specify):

SOCIAL INTERACTION	How You Describe Yourself
Friends	a. I enjoy hanging out in big groups. b. I lean towards one-on-one interactions or solitude (if it's the latter, you've found the perfect guideline!). c. Others (specify):
Family	a. I try to spend time with my family whenever possible. b. I only meet up with my family when it's necessary. c. Others (specify):
Conversation	a. I enjoy delving into various subjects in depth. b. I tend to be concise in my communication. c. Others (specify):

Notes/insights from the above:

_____

_____

_____

_____

_____

_____

_____

_____

TRY THIS: Make Use Of Your Time Alone

Got some ideas for something fresh you'd like to trial? Here are three different ways to spend solo time and use it as an opportunity to delve deeper into self-discovery. Choose the option below that piques your interest the most—since part of this is about uncovering your own preferences—or feel free to come up with your own.

1. Take on a new skill that requires weeks, months, or even longer to master. Maybe it's those long-desired singing lessons, learning how to roller skate, or joining the bandwagon and finally diving into the art of baking sourdough. What attracted you to this particular skill? Why did you wait until now to pursue it? How does acquiring this new skill impact your self-assurance and self-value? Does it align with your perception of your identity and the person you aspire to be? It's perfectly fine to seek guidance from an instructor, such as a music teacher if you opt for a musical instrument. The main goal is to create an opportunity for introspection in solitude, discovering what the new activity reveals about yourself.

Reflection:

2. Embark on a solo journey. Discover more about yourself as you plan a weekend getaway that you'll experience alone. You'll swiftly realize your level of independence. This is an excellent exercise, particularly if you harbor fears of solitude.

Are you:

- Torn between options/able to make decisions
- Minimalist/one who packs a lot
- Chill/on the go
- Satisfied/uninterested
- Tidy/disorganized
- Structured/unpredictable
- Do you engage in inner dialogue or experience a tranquil mind?
- Are you certain or do you second-guess your decisions?
- Do you feel self-aware or self-assured?
- What aspects of traveling captivate you the most?
- Which destination piques your interest for your next adventure?

Reflection:

_____

_____

_____

_____

_____

_____

_____

_____

3. Try your hand at a task you've never tackled before. It may be challenging to squeeze it in if you already have a full-time job, but if you can make it work, give a different kind of work a shot. Offer your services as a volunteer at a library, sign up as a driver for a ride-share service, wait tables, babysit, or even take up teaching. It's important to note that while many of these options involve interacting with others, the key is that you undertake them independently, you embark on them alone, and you reflect on the experience in solitude.

- Which aspects of your personality remain unchanged regardless of your actions?
- What revelations about yourself do you uncover?
- Is it the intrigue surrounding this job or the additional income that holds greater significance for you?
- Do you enjoy socializing with others or working autonomously?
- Do you prefer receiving explicit instructions or figuring things out on your own?
- Are you more inclined to seek permission or seek forgiveness?
- Does work energize or drain you?
- Do you desire to broaden this newfound opportunity in your life?

Reflection:

_____

_____

_____

_____

_____

_____

_____

TRY THIS: Identify Your Biggest Growth Area

Now, let's examine your life from all angles, exploring these five key aspects: Personal, Financial, Mental/Emotional, Physical Health, and Relationships. Select the option that best describes your connection with each of these areas. Once you've finished the questionnaire, assess your current position and contemplate where you aspire to be. Which area holds the greatest potential for personal growth?

1. Personality
     a. I'm not a fan of myself.
     b. I enjoy myself when others approve of me.
     c. I value myself despite my imperfections and strive for personal growth.

     ☐ OKAY WITH WHERE I AM
     ☐ WANT TO CHANGE

2. Emotional Health
     a. I frequently experience unease and restlessness.
     b. I suppress my emotions to accomplish tasks.
     c. I acknowledge my emotions and make an effort to work through them.

     ☐ OKAY WITH WHERE I AM
     ☐ WANT TO CHANGE

3. Physical Health
     a. I neglect my body, or I dislike it.
     b. I actively prioritize my physical appearance because it matters to me.
     c. I take care of myself and appreciate my body.

     ☐ OKAY WITH WHERE I AM
     ☐ WANT TO CHANGE

4. Relationships
     a. I feel insecure about certain relationships.
     b. My happiness relies on my relationships.
     c. I invest in my relationships to foster their growth.

     ☐ OKAY WITH WHERE I AM
     ☐ WANT TO CHANGE

5. Money
> a. Contemplating money fills me with worry and anxiety.
> b. Thinking about money evokes excitement and ambition. I envy those with more wealth than I possess.
> c. Considering money brings contentment. If anything, I desire more to be able to give more.

☐ OKAY WITH WHERE I AM
☐ WANT TO CHANGE

Let's say the most significant area for improvement you've recognized is your finances. Overspending has consistently posed a challenge for you. When you have personal time, it's essential to concentrate on taking action in this specific domain. While I could go into great detail about developing and attaining goals, a practical approach to begin is by crafting a growth strategy utilizing the three Cs of transformation:

1. *Coaching.* In our modern world, accessing experts and information is incredibly convenient. Begin by exploring readily available resources that can assist you with this matter. Seek out a book, podcast, course, buddy, professional, TED Talk, MasterClass, or online video that can provide guidance. You'll discover that most of these resources offer strategies to break down your objective into smaller, attainable steps, thereby bringing clarity to a challenge that once seemed overwhelming.

2. *Consistency.* Utilize the gathered information to devise a plan for addressing the issue consistently over time. Set a goal for the end of the year, but ensure that it revolves around taking action rather than solely achieving an outcome. Instead of aiming for something like "Make a million dollars," focus on committing to continuous efforts that foster personal growth in this particular area.

3. *Community.* Seek out a community that can offer support and aid your endeavors. There are online and local groups available for virtually any interest. Look for one where you can find a diverse mix of individuals who share your circumstances, those who are in the process of making changes, and those who have already achieved some level of success in transforming their lives in a manner aligned with your aspirations. Consider whether you prefer a community that provides motivation, information, or a blend of both. Who knows? You might even encounter your future partner in such a community.

Notes/insights from the above:

_____

_____

_____

_____

_____

_____

_____

_____

RULE 2: DON'T IGNORE YOUR KARMA

TRY THIS: Younger-Self Meditation

Take a moment to discover the imprints left by your past and gain insight into how they shape your perception of love. The purpose is not to blame others or idealize them, but rather to identify the emotional patterns that influenced you during your formative years.

Think of this introspection as an adventurous excavation of yourself. There are hidden artifacts waiting to be unearthed—some precious, some partially exposed, and some insignificant. They reveal the complexities and scars of bygone years and offer valuable lessons about life.

Delve into unresolved and unfulfilled desires by reconnecting with your thirteen- or fourteen-year-old self. Provide your younger self with the words, wisdom, and affection they long for. Embrace your younger self and consider what they needed to hear but were never told.

- You look amazing.
- You're brave.
- Have faith in yourself.
- Everything will be fine.
- You're not foolish.

How would your younger self react to these words?
- Thanks for coming back to share this with me.
- Don't get too worked up.
- You should consider getting back into singing.

Once you've had this discussion with your younger self, give them a warm hug and express gratitude for their valuable perspective.

Notes/insights from the above:

_____

_____

_____

_____

TRY THIS: Identify Parental Gifts And Gaps

MEMORIES

Jot down three of your most cherished recollections from your early years.

_____

_____

_____

Jot down three of the most unpleasant recollections you have from your early years.

_____

_____

_____

Recall a difficult period from your early years. Did your parents provide assistance during that time? In what ways? How did it impact you?

_____

_____

_____

_____

The responses you received from your parents may not have been straightforward. A caring reaction could have provided comfort or could have led to dependency. A harsh reaction might have affected your self-confidence or strengthened your resilience. What's important is not whether your parents were the greatest parents ever, but rather how their treatment of you influenced your growth.

EXPECTATIONS

What kind of expectations did your parents hold for you? Did these expectations serve as motivation or put pressure on you? How do they impact your relationships?

If your parents had specific expectations regarding your achievements or the type of partner you should have, you might find yourself excessively attached to those outcomes or rebelling against them. How are these influences still affecting your life? I once knew someone whose parents constantly emphasized the importance of marrying an ambitious individual, but her previous boyfriend ended their relationship by stating, "I don't want to be your business partner; I want to be your boyfriend." She had to release her parents' desires for her and reevaluate her own criteria for a genuine partner.

Reflection:

_____

_____

_____

_____

_____

_____

_____

MODELING

Which aspects of a relationship did your parents demonstrate that you found appealing/unappealing?

Frequently, we tend to either reject or replicate the patterns set by our parents in our own relationships. For instance, if they engaged in arguments, you might steer clear of conflicts. If they had a particular power dynamic, you might anticipate the same in your own relationship or actively avoid it.

Reflection:

_____

_____

_____

_____

_____

EMOTIONAL SUPPORT

What sort of love and emotional encouragement do you wish your parents had bestowed upon you? What experiences or aspects did you feel were missingtim?

Once you recognize a blessing or deficiency that affects your relationships, you can begin to tackle it.

1. *Recognize.* The initial step is to identify the situations and circumstances where that feeling leads you astray. Does it arise from social media? Specific social circles? Celebrations with your partner? Travel experiences?

2. *Remind yourself.* Reinforce your desired behavior or avoid unwanted behavior by setting reminders. These reminders should catch you in those critical moments when you're at risk of acting in a way you'd rather not. For instance, if you anticipate needing support that your partner doesn't typically provide, or if you feel jealous when you see your partner interacting in groups, or if a certain behavior always triggers your anger, find a way to remind yourself in advance that you want to change in that particular moment, time, and space. It could be as simple as sticking a Post-it Note on your bathroom mirror, writing a note in your journal, or asking your partner to remind you of what you're currently working on.

3. *Repeat.* Transform your reminder into a mantra, a phrase that you repeat to yourself repeatedly. By doing so, it's more likely to come to your mind at the precise moment when you need it. It could be something like "Love is without guilt" or "Anger isn't the solution" or "Ask before assuming."

4. *Reduce.* As you consistently reinforce your desired behavior, you'll gradually find yourself indulging in negative reactions or expectations less frequently. Keep your partner informed about your efforts so that they understand you're actively working on reducing those habits.

5. *Remove.* Eventually, with sustained focus and repetition, you'll break the habit of expecting certain outcomes entirely.

Reflection:

_____

_____

_____

_____

_____

_____

_____

_____

TRY THIS: Media Love

Recall the initial instance when you encountered a love song or watched a movie that influenced or altered your perception of love. What qualities of love did it depict? Do you believe in those qualities? Have you experienced them in your past romantic connections?

Examples:
- You had me at hello—Jerry Maguire
- I wish I knew how to quit you—Brokeback Mountain
- To me, you are perfect—Love Actually
- As you wish—The Princess Bride
- You want the moon? Just say the word, and I'll throw a lasso around it and pull it down—It's a Wonderful Life
- I'm also just a girl, standing in front of a boy, asking him to love her—Notting Hill

Once we grasp the imprints that media has left on our perceptions of love stories, we become less reliant on Hollywood's idea of perfection in our own relationships. We become open to the possibility of a love that unfolds gradually or takes a different path.

Notes/insights from the above:

_____

_____

_____

_____

_____

_____

_____

TRY THIS: Relationship Roles

Let's define and explore the role(s) you played in your most recent relationship or anticipate having in a future relationship. Does it / do they align with your desires? While you'll experience all the roles mentioned below, the goal is to progress towards becoming mutual supporters, while also embracing occasional moments of problem-solving and dependency.

TYPE 1: FIXER

Were you always caught up in the never-ending cycle of attempting to resolve, support, assist, or enhance the other person? Were you shouldering the burden of carrying them and working towards achieving their goals on their behalf?

_____

_____

_____

_____

_____

TYPE 2: DEPENDENT

Did you ever have the sense that you depended excessively on your significant other? Did you constantly turn to them for every problem you faced, anticipating them to come up with solutions?

_____

_____

_____

_____

_____

TYPE 3: SUPPORTER

Did their personality resonate with you, did you value their beliefs, and did you feel inclined to support them in achieving their aspirations? Did you appreciate their time management and the way they maintained their personal environment, or did you constantly want them to alter it?

_____

_____

_____

_____

_____

The fixer adopts a parental mindset. You feel responsible for looking after the other person and nurturing them. Their happiness becomes your top priority. While this mentality can be beneficial, it can also become excessive. When you assume the role of a parent to your partner, it encourages them to behave like a child.

The dependent possesses a childlike mentality. You depend on your partner, wanting them to solve all your problems, and you become upset when they can't provide all the answers. Sometimes, we adopt this mindset when we have a controlling partner. It can be comforting to have someone else take charge. However, we miss out on shaping our own lives and following our own path.

The supporter stands by their partner as their champion. You are neither a parent nor a child; you stand side by side with your partner. You take responsibility, develop patience, and aim to help the other person grow without trying to micromanage them. This balanced approach can be likened to the "just right" mentality, like Goldilocks.

For a quiz that can help identify the role you play in your relationship, please visit www.RelationshipRoles.com.

It's natural for us to transition between these three roles in our relationships. Sometimes we take the lead, while other times we are more comfortable following. The goal is to avoid being stuck in the same dynamic with a specific type all the time.

Being a full-time fixer means your partner isn't embarking on their own journey, and it's not our place to undertake it for them. We shouldn't try to fix something that may not even be broken. Being consistently fragile means lacking confidence and seeking validation from others. You feel broken and desire someone to fix you. Being with a partner who perpetuates this side of you hinders taking responsibility for your own growth, joy, and success.

Striving to be a supporter is an ideal goal. Both partners communicate as equals, always learning from each other. When both parties recognize that they are simultaneously teaching and learning, a true partnership is formed. (More on this in Rule 3.)

TRY THIS: Reflect And Learn From A Past Relationship

When it comes to relationships, we often measure success by their duration, but their true worth resides in the lessons and personal growth they offer. Recognizing this, we can analyze the decisions we've made, understand the reasons behind our choices of partners, identify where things went awry, and gain a clearer understanding of whom to choose and whether any changes are necessary for future connections.

1. What energy were you in when you decided to be with your former partner?

Energy of ignorance. In this energy, you may have chosen someone out of boredom, limited options, or a sense of loneliness. Decisions made in cluelessness often result in feelings of sadness, pain, and stress.

Energy of passion. In this energy, you selected someone because you desired one of the luxuries they offered. Choices made in enthusiasm may start off well, but they need to evolve into understanding and respect to avoid a terrible ending.

Energy of goodness. In this energy, you opted for someone with whom you felt a connection and compatibility. There was mutual respect, and often these relationships conclude with some lingering feelings of respect.

_____

_____

_____

_____

2. Why did it come to an end? Try to be completely truthful with yourself as you evaluate what went awry in this relationship.

_____

_____

_____

_____

_____

_____

3. Take lessons from it. What ideas come to mind regarding what you'll attempt to do differently in the future? Is it possible for you to approach your next relationship with a positive mindset? Can you set aside material possessions and focus on identifying qualities that make for great partners?

_____

_____

_____

_____

_____

_____

_____

TRY THIS: What You Showcase

When there's a difference between what captivates your partner and what you cherish about yourself, you might find it challenging to meet their expectations. To begin with, jot down a catalog of the things you love about yourself. Reflect on the qualities that make you proud, avoiding any exaggerations. Are you kind, compassionate, diligent, genuine, imaginative, appreciative, adaptable, or dependable?

Now, for each of your significant or defining relationships, compile a list of the qualities you believe those individuals recognized and valued in you. Our aim is to cultivate relationships where we are cherished for the aspects we appreciate in ourselves.

Qualities I love about myself:

_____

_____

_____

Qualities My Partner Loves About Me

    Relationship #1:

    _____

    _____

    _____

    Relationship #2:

    _____

    _____

    _____

Relationship #3:

_____

_____

_____

Relationship #4:

_____

_____

_____

Relationship #5:

_____

_____

_____

TRY THIS: Give Yourself What You Want To Receive

Fill your own gaps by looking for ways to treat yourself the way you're looking for others to treat you.

Examples:

I never felt valued by my parents.
If you want to be acknowledged...
What aspects do you seek recognition for?
What daily actions can make you feel valued?

_____

_____

_____

_____

I always felt like my parents didn't see me as unique.
If you desire to feel extraordinary...
What aspect would you like to be seen as extraordinary for?
What daily actions can you take to cultivate a sense of uniqueness within yourself?

_____

_____

_____

_____

My folks didn't value my emotions or viewpoints.
If you desire a sense of respect...
What aspects do you seek respect for?
What actions can you take daily to honor yourself?

_____

_____

_____

_____

_____

These questions can be challenging, so take your time contemplating them. The answers may not come easily. Reflect on them for a day, maybe even a week. Gradually, you might begin to recognize recurring negative thoughts that stem from your past.

If you constantly reinforce the belief that you're nobody unless someone validates you, it will lead to increased insecurity, stress, and pressure. Similarly, if you frequently convince yourself that you're not adequate, you will indeed feel inadequate.

To break free from these negative patterns, we must cultivate new thought patterns. It might feel artificial or forced at first, but as you practice these fresh, positive thoughts, you'll find yourself embodying them.

Part Two: Compatibility: Learning To Love Others

RULE 3: DEFINE LOVE BEFORE YOU THINK IT, FEEL IT, OR SAY IT

TRY THIS: Prepare For Date One

Go ahead and answer the questions I proposed for you to ask your date, but this time, write down your own responses.

What's an activity that brings you joy?

_____

_____

Do you have a favorite place?

_____

_____

Have you come across a book or movie that you've revisited multiple times?

_____

_____

What's on your mind the most right now?

_____

_____

Is there something you're curious to learn more about?

_____

_____

What's the most amazing meal you've ever experienced?

_____

_____

After gathering your responses, reflect on what they could potentially reveal about you. Do these questions touch upon your passionate interests? Do they provide an opportunity to showcase significant aspects of your personality? If not, consider if there are alternative questions that could accomplish this. Include those questions in the list you bring along for your upcoming date.

TRY THIS: Set A Schedule

Let's figure out the frequency of your communication, messaging, and meetings as a couple. Find a comfortable and balanced rhythm that suits both of you. Determine how you'd like to distribute your free time. It's not necessary for every week to be identical, but having an idea of how you'll spend your time helps avoid feeling like you're competing with other interests.

- Evenings alone
- Evenings spent together
- Evenings with shared friends or family
- Evenings with your own friends

Notes/insights from the above:

_____

_____

_____

_____

_____

_____

TRY THIS: Daily Trust

One of the ways I love demonstrating trust every day is by acknowledging and appreciating when someone follows through on a promise. Often, we express gratitude and thanks when people surprise us with a kind gesture. For instance, when your partner unexpectedly prepares a delicious dinner, we shower them with appreciation. The same goes for when they do something out of the ordinary. However, trust is also built on consistent reliability. What about the partner who regularly makes dinner for us? It's important to show our gratitude for their daily efforts. The more we acknowledge and reward it, the more likely they are to continue. Similarly, we can build their trust in us by consistently showing up.

This week, let's make a conscious effort to express gratitude to our partners for the consistent effort and energy they bring to our relationship. Be specific in your appreciation. Instead of a generic "Thanks for listening," you can say, "I know I often come home and unload my work-related emotions on you. I genuinely appreciate how you listen attentively and provide me with valuable advice."

Notes/insights from the above:

_____

_____

_____

_____

_____

_____

_____

TRY THIS: Build Realistic Dreams Together

Make it a habit to have a monthly catch-up session. Dedicate an hour each month to have a conversation about your relationship. This allows you to confirm what aspects are going smoothly and make adjustments where necessary.

Pinpoint a positive moment. What are you appreciative of? This helps both of you recognize the things that are going positively.

_____

_____

Pinpoint a hurdle. What's giving you a tough time? This allows you to recognize areas that require improvement.

_____

_____

Discover a joint goal to pursue in the upcoming month. It could be a special night out, a birthday bash, a getaway, or a plan to renovate a room in your home. Browse an online platform to explore vacation options that interest you. By doing so, you'll be co-creating your aspirations. Together, you'll be actively shaping the desired look and atmosphere of your relationship.

Notes/insights from the above:

_____

_____

_____

_____

RULE 4: YOUR PARTNER IS YOUR GURU

TRY THIS: Assess Whether Your Partner Is Someone You Can Learn And Grow With

Even in the early stages of getting to know someone, we can detect indications that go beyond mere enjoyment of their company and suggest their potential as a suitable partner for personal growth. By pondering these questions, you'll be amazed at the extent of your existing knowledge regarding your partner's ability to embark on a learning journey alongside you.

For each question, rate whether your partner does it always, sometimes, or never.

1. *Do they like learning about themselves?* If someone lacks curiosity about discovering themselves, they might find it challenging to understand you. If someone possesses a strong desire for personal growth, they will also support your growth. Do they enjoy exploring new experiences? Are they self-reflective? Are they open to therapy, coaching, or other avenues of personal development? Do they value conversations about decision-making and choices?
   - ☐ ALWAYS
   - ☐ SOMETIMES
   - ☐ NEVER

2. *Do they understand their own emotions?* Does your partner excel at comprehending and conveying their emotions? Do they merely skim the surface when discussing their day, or do they genuinely open up and share their emotions? When they recount a story, do they incorporate their emotional state into it?
   - ☐ ALWAYS
   - ☐ SOMETIMES
   - ☐ NEVER

3. *Do they try to understand you?* Do they show an interest in getting to know you? Having self-awareness often, though not always, leads to a sense of curiosity about others. Do they utilize their emotional intelligence to gain a deeper understanding of who you are? If they haven't reached a stage where they can broaden their capacity for care and love, it suggests they are still in the phase of self-exploration. They are still focused on their personal growth and not prepared to embark on a shared learning journey with you.
   - ☐ ALWAYS
   - ☐ SOMETIMES
   - ☐ NEVER

4. Can they entertain themselves? Having a companion who appreciates solitude makes learning together easier. It signifies that they have their own unique journey and path, enabling you to walk alongside them while pursuing your own path.

☐ ALWAYS
☐ SOMETIMES
☐ NEVER

5. Are they open to finding new ways of solving problems? For instance, when they encounter difficulties with a coworker, do they confide in you or a friend? Are they open to discussing the issue with the colleague, suggesting a compromise, or changing the approach by inviting them for a lunch meeting? Embracing learning and personal growth entails possessing the resolve and adaptability to tackle problems from fresh perspectives. This mindset can also be applied to relationships.

☐ ALWAYS
☐ SOMETIMES
☐ NEVER

6. Do they support others in their growth? Take notice of whether they put in the effort to assist a friend, a sibling, or a mentee. Do they actively engage in helping others? This demonstrates their ability to expand their capacity for love and care, which is essential in the concept of Grhastha.

☐ ALWAYS
☐ SOMETIMES
☐ NEVER

7. Do they inspire you to be better and more? Having a partner can ignite your ambition, not to seek their approval, but because they have faith in your capabilities and empower you to pursue your passions and inclinations with confidence.

☐ ALWAYS
☐ SOMETIMES
☐ NEVER

The outcomes of this assessment do not determine the fate of your relationship. Take a look at the questions where you answered "never" or "sometimes." These indicate the areas where you should take the initiative. If your partner rarely spends time alone, you should either accept this or find ways to encourage them to engage in solitary activities that interest them. You can brainstorm activities that facilitate self-reflection (check out the TRY THIS exercises in Rule 1).

Alternatively, if your partner lacks self-awareness, it might affect your relationship. In such cases, gently educate them about your own needs and preferences, saying something like, "I tend to be more irritable after work, so let's tackle our finances on the weekend."

When we enroll in a class or book an Airbnb, we conduct research before committing. Similarly, exercises like this serve as research into our relationship. Even if a partner doesn't fulfill all the criteria, they can still evolve into someone with whom you can learn and grow, as long as you both remain open to teaching and learning from each other.

Notes/insights from the above:

_____

_____

_____

_____

_____

_____

_____

_____

_____

TRY THIS: Help Your Partner Know Their Goals

Rather than dictating your partner's goals and methods for achieving them, try posing three questions to them.

1. What's truly significant to you at this moment?

_____

_____

2. What is necessary for you to reach that point?

_____

_____

3. Do you need any assistance from me?

_____

_____

This approach allows your partner to navigate their own path towards finding answers. Offering the gift of understanding their goals without altering them to align with your own is truly valuable. When we hear about someone else's aspirations, we often filter and interpret them based on our own perspective. We might deem them too small or too grand. While your viewpoint matters, it's important not to impose or anticipate. We shouldn't impose our own limitations or aspirations on them. Be sure to actively listen to their reasons, what drives them, and why. You'll also gain insights and learn from this process.

Notes/insights from the above:

_____

_____

_____

_____

TRY THIS: Identify Your Partner's Learning Style
Which learning style most accurately characterizes your partner?
- *Hearing.* Your partner prefers absorbing new information through their sense of hearing. They enjoy listening to podcasts, audiobooks, or TED Talks.
- *Vision.* Your partner finds it effective to observe someone demonstrating a skill or follow a diagram. They learn best from platforms like YouTube or MasterClass.
- *Thought.* Your partner absorbs information by engaging their thoughts. They may prefer reading a book on a topic of interest and taking notes to express it in their own words.
- *Motion.* Your partner learns through hands-on experience. They would be interested in attending workshops where they can actively practice and develop new skills.

Identify your partner's learning style by asking them if they are aware of their preferred method of learning. If they are unsure, inquire about the last time they learned something new and how they received the information. If you're still uncertain, pay attention to how they spend their free time. Do they watch documentaries or listen to audiobooks? You can even assist them in exploring various approaches and discovering their preference.

Provide guidance on how to learn using the suggested formats for each learning style mentioned above. Consider gifting them something inspiring, conducting research on their behalf, or engaging in joint experiments. Seek creative ways to share ideas with your partner as a guru, rather than imposing or pressuring them.

Notes/insights from the above:

_____

_____

_____

_____

_____

TRY THIS: Appreciate Your Partner's Knowledge

The next time you engage in conversation with your partner, make a point to recognize an area of expertise they possess, which you tend to overlook. How can you discover something remarkable in what you already know about your partner?

Perhaps they have a habit of thoughtful decision-making. Maybe they consistently write heartfelt thank-you notes. It could be that they consistently provide you with valuable advice even when you're unsure of how to ask for help at work.

Take note of the skills your partner possesses that you have never acknowledged before. Once you identify one, express your appreciation to them. This act of recognition will nourish and uplift your partner's strengths.

Notes/insights from the above:

_____

_____

_____

_____

_____

TRY THIS: Introduce A New Idea

Improve your communication abilities by initiating a conversation about a fresh subject and actively paying attention to your partner's words. Listen to the ideas they express and assist them in uncovering and expressing the emotions, desires, and needs underlying their words.

Choose a topic that allows for open-ended discussions and hasn't been explored before. Opt for something that can spark imagination and inspire both of you to consider new possibilities for shared activities.

How about considering these ideas:

- Imagine if we both walked away from our jobs and relocated?
- What if we embarked on a year-long adventure of traveling?
- If we were able to retire one day, how would we choose to spend our time?
- If we suddenly had a million dollars to donate, who would we choose to give it to and what would be our reasons?

Let's delve into some thought-provoking queries (both of you can answer these questions, but make sure to actively listen to your partner's responses):

- What's the immediate thought that pops into your head when I pose this question?
- What is it about your response that resonates with you?

Next, demonstrate to your partner that you have understood them:

- Share with them your understanding of their proposed idea.
- Engage in a conversation about the preferences and priorities that you believe might be behind their idea.
- Express what you have discovered about them through this discussion.
- Explore the possibility of incorporating a feasible version of their desired outcome into your lives at present.

_____

_____

_____

_____

For instance:

If the question was about how you would spend a year traveling, you might have a strong inclination to relocate to the southern region of France and indulge in pain au chocolat for an entire year. However, your partner has a different idea and wants to organize a cross-country bike adventure across the United States. It's important to acknowledge their yearning for physical activity. Perhaps they also wish to embrace a slower pace of travel or spend time camping along the route. Once you have a better understanding of their aspirations, you could consider surprising them with a bike as a birthday gift. Alternatively, you may plan a weekend getaway focused on cycling together.

This exercise serves as a practice for actively listening to your partner rather than merely listening to formulate a response, especially when dealing with more challenging and emotionally charged topics.

Notes/insights from the above:

_____

_____

_____

TRY THIS: Acknowledge The Guru's Skills

Reflect on your partner's abilities as a wise mentor. What are their strong points? Have you taken a moment to appreciate them? And if you view certain aspects as shortcomings, is there something you can discover about yourself based on your reaction? Identify the domains where your partner serves as your mentor and express gratitude towards them. You can unexpectedly show your appreciation or do so the next time they exhibit these qualities.

1. Leads through service

Your significant other is ready to take on any role to assist you, even if it's not their area of expertise. They might act as a manager, an accountant, an IT technician, or even a food delivery person. Are they providing assistance out of genuine care rather than dictating what you should do?

2. Leads by example

What are the things they consistently commit to and never fail to do? If you're unable to find anything, chances are you haven't dug deep enough.

3. Helps you to your goals, not theirs

Your significant other enables you to embrace your true self. They don't compel or pressure you to change. While they may not be actively serving or assisting you, their non-demanding nature and acceptance of who you are is a form of support.

4. Offers guidance without criticism, judgment, or abuse

When you haven't achieved your goals or made an error, your partner stands by you, providing support and encouragement without imposing any pressure. It's important to recognize the qualities of a student as well. You can apply the same approach to assessing those qualities.

Notes/insights from the above:

_____

_____

_____

_____

_____

RULE 5: PURPOSE COMES FIRST

TRY THIS: Learn About Your Purpose

Discovering our purpose comes from reflecting on and delving into our passions and abilities.

PASSIONS

Take a moment to inquire about your passions.

- If you could earn money by pursuing any activity, what would it be?
- Are there hobbies you adored as a child but no longer engage in?
- Do you possess a secret skill?
- Have you come across someone who has the job you've always dreamt of?
- Is there something you would be doing if you weren't constrained by your location or circumstances?
- Is there something you were once skilled at but now miss?
- Is there a talent you haven't had the opportunity to pursue recently?

My Passions:

_____

_____

_____

_____

_____

STRENGTHS

Discover the roles you assume in your home or workplace to uncover your areas of expertise.

- *The organizer*: The planner takes charge of birthdays and vacations and ensures life runs smoothly. The coordinator prioritizes deadlines, outcomes, and the overall perspective. You excel at guiding others.
- *The energizer*: Full of energy, enthusiasm, and positivity, the sparkplug ignites excitement among people, motivating them to embark on the activities planned by the coordinator.

- *The empathizer*: With emotional intelligence, patience, attentive listening, and supportive nature, the empathic individual possesses an intuitive understanding of others' emotions.
- *The analyzer*: With a keen eye for detail, a systematic approach, carefulness, and caution, the analyzer identifies potential issues that may pose problems in the future.

My Strengths:

_____

_____

_____

_____

YOUR PURPOSE IS WHERE YOUR PASSIONS INTERSECT WITH YOUR SKILLS.
Once you've pinpointed your passions and abilities, explore avenues to expand your knowledge about them.

1. Enroll in a course, delve into a book, or tune in to a podcast related to your field of interest. Is there a certification program available that can enhance your talent?

2. Seek out communities or collectives of individuals who can inspire you with their actions or approaches.

3. Dedicate your weekends to experimenting with activities aligned with your purpose. Pay attention to what sparks excitement and further ignites your interests.

Notes/insights from the above:

_____

_____

_____

_____

TRY THIS: Meet With A Mentor

1. SEEK OUT POSSIBLE MENTORS.

Utilize your current network to establish connections with individuals who have expertise in your area of interest.

Engage with them through social media platforms.

Review the learning materials you've used, such as books, TED Talks, podcasts, etc., and follow up to inquire if those who could provide valuable guidance would be open to sparing just ten minutes for your inquiries.

2. INQUIRE AND TAKE NOTE OF THEIR ANSWERS.

Commence by asking straightforward, strategic, and hands-on queries like:
- How did you begin?
- What steps did you take to enhance your skills?
- Which methods do you employ?
- Are there any individuals you collaborate with?
  And any other inquiries regarding their process.

Notes from mentors:

_____

_____

_____

_____

_____

Feel free to be detailed in your inquiries. If you don't ask specific questions, you won't receive specific answers.

You can also inquire about emotional and mental aspects that can provide insights into what you might enjoy about the process and what challenges you may encounter.

- Which aspect of the process brings you the most enjoyment?
- What do you dislike about the process?
- What do you wish you had been aware of when you initially began?

Notes from mentors:

_____

_____

_____

_____

_____

3. PROCESS.

Once you've had a conversation with a mentor, take a glance at your notes. Are there individuals you need to reach out to? Abilities you should work on? Opportunities you should seize? Transform the advice and insights you received into actionable tasks and schedule them accordingly on your calendar.

Notes From Mentor	Action Plan

TRY THIS: Spare Time Worksheet

You have the opportunity to reclaim lost time by documenting each minute of your day and grouping tasks together, similar to Schulte's method. However, this exercise offers a simpler approach by examining whether the time we invest aligns with our values.

Discover your true values by dedicating a consistent portion of your leisure time to learning within your area of purpose. Together with your partner, assess how you currently spend your free time, both individually and together. This exercise not only provides insight into your values but also allows you to consider any desired changes to your leisure activities.

To begin, like in the example chart provided, determine the overall number of hours you dedicate to the activities mentioned and any additional ones you wish to include each week. Next, in the second column, calculate the amount of time you're open to **subtracting** from those activities and **reallocating** it towards exploring your purpose.

Activities I Enjoy	Time I Currently Spend	Time I Will Now Commit To Spend
Refueling/pure leisure	4 hours/week	3 hours/week
Exercise	4 hours/week	4 hours/week (no change)
Socializing	8 hours/week	7 hours/week
Entertainment	15 hours/week	10 hours/week
Total time spent on activities that are not my purpose	31 total hours	24 total hours (I have freed up seven hours per week)
Learning about my purpose	0 hours	7 hours

Activities I Enjoy	Time I Currently Spend	Time I Will Now Commit To Spend

Involve your partner in this endeavor. If you don't share your enthusiasm for what you want to pursue, they might question why you're not interested in spending time together. If they're on board with this idea, they will comprehend and honor your choices regarding how you spend your time.

TRY THIS: Set Goals Together

Once a year, set aside some time to have a conversation with your partner about your aspirations and objectives. Just like maintaining a home, you need to keep your goals in check. Each year, you clean the gutters, replace smoke alarm batteries, and take care of repairs. Similarly, in a relationship, it's essential to evaluate your purpose and how both of you perceive your progress towards it. You can have individual dreams and a shared dream. For instance, your personal goal might involve learning to paint, while your partner's ambition could be mastering web design. And together, you might aim to learn how to dance.

What are you striving to accomplish? Are you working towards acquiring skills that align with your purpose? Are you seeking a job that is more closely connected to your goals? Are you trying to carve out more time for your purpose?

What do you expect from your partner? How can they support you in fulfilling your purpose? Do you need emotional encouragement? Would you like them to assist you with other responsibilities, allowing you more time for your own purpose?

What does your partner desire from you? Do you believe in their purpose? How can you support and encourage them in pursuing their aspirations?

Similar to the regular maintenance tasks of a home, there are also more frequent issues that need addressing beyond the once-a-year check-in. You pay monthly bills, change a lightbulb when it burns out, or fix a leak. If challenges arise for you or your partner, make sure to discuss them together.

Before you sit down with your partner for this exercise, consider how you plan to approach it. Presenting it as, "Jay Shetty said we should answer these questions about our purpose every year. Let's do it now," may not yield great results. Similarly, adopting an evangelical preacher's tone may not be effective. Avoid rushing to your partner to introduce a new frequency or mode of communication. First, internalize these ideas on your own. Begin quietly supporting your partner's purpose instead of announcing your intentions. Observe the impact it has on you, your partner, and your relationship. Then, share your observations with your partner using a communication style that you know works well for them.

Notes/insights from the above:

_____

_____

_____

_____

_____

_____

_____

_____

_____

_____

_____

_____

_____

_____

TRY THIS: Adjust A Dharma Imbalance

When your partner's life purpose becomes all-encompassing in the relationship, you can follow a similar process to the one I described earlier for dealing with a struggling partner. Here's what you can do:

1. Prioritize your own purpose. When you feel frustrated with your partner's purpose, it's crucial to focus on your own. This ensures that you don't make your partner's purpose your sole focus.

2. Engage in open communication. Have a discussion about why you both are finding it challenging to make time for each other. Remember, you shouldn't be competing with your partner's purpose for their time. Instead, emphasize the importance of their presence in your relationship.

3. Make commitments and agreements. Together, determine how much time each of you will dedicate to your respective purposes and establish designated family time. Set boundaries and make a sincere commitment to adhere to them.

4. Identify shared activities that enhance the value of your time together as a couple or family. For instance, rather than simply watching TV, find interactive activities that you both enjoy. On weekends, engage in physically active pursuits like hiking or a sport that appeals to both of you. Consider entertaining friends or family, volunteering, or engaging in activities that promote learning and discussion. On weekdays, when time is limited, you can play games, cook together, or explore educational content that aligns with the purposes you both cherish. If you have the energy, you can plan additional activities like listening to music or attending a lecture together or try out something entirely new.

5. Establish a timeline to review and assess the effectiveness of the new plan. Determine when you would like to reconnect to ensure that you're honoring your agreements or if any adjustments need to be made along the way.

Notes/insights from the above:

_____

_____

_____

_____

TRY THIS: Do A Time Trade

You and your partner have the opportunity to alleviate the pressure of two hectic lives by exchanging the gift of time. Here are a few suggestions for trading time commitments with your partner:

- Assume a responsibility that is typically handled by your partner, either temporarily or permanently.
- Devise an activity that allows you to step aside (along with everyone else) and create space for your partner.
- Clear your evening schedule for an entire weekend and prioritize the partner who requires more time for their goals.
- Choose a holiday and dedicate it entirely to the partner who needs some extra time.

Notes/insights from the above:

_____

_____

_____

_____

_____

_____

_____

_____

Part Three: Healing: Learning To Love Through Struggle

RULE 6: EGO – WIN OR LOSE TOGETHER

TRY THIS: Shift An Argument To A Shared Goal

Rather than viewing it as a situation where you're pitted against each other, approach the conversation as a joint effort between the two of you to tackle the problem. When we approach the situation as adversaries, the chances of a fight escalate. Come to the table as a united team ready to face the problem together.

Check out these instances of how you can redirect a disagreement towards a common objective. In the upcoming section are ways for you to proactively strategize and ensure that your conflicts yield productive outcomes.

Argument	Reframe/Shared Goal
"You don't clean up after yourself."	"We should set a routine for daily chores."
"You're always late."	"Can we sit down and talk about how we want to spend our time in the evenings and on weekends?"
"You don't mind spending money on your interests but complain when I spend money on mine."	"Let's set a reasonable monthly budget."
"You don't give the children as much attention as they need from you."	"Let's discuss what we think the children need [maybe with them, depending on their ages] and how we can support that."

Argument	Reframe/Shared Goal

TRY THIS: Identify Your Ego And Passion In The Conflict

Determine whether your disagreement is meaningless (lack of knowledge), driven by power (intense emotions), or constructive (positive intentions).

1. Jot down the significance of the matter to you. What triggered your anger?
2. Determine your motivation for standing up:

- Am I arguing because I think my way is superior? (ego)
- Am I arguing because I believe there is a correct way to do things? (ego)
- Am I arguing because I want the person to change? (passion)
- Am I arguing because this situation deeply upsets me? (passion)
- Am I arguing because I seek a sense of novelty? (passion)
- Am I arguing because I aim to enhance the situation? (goodness)
- Am I arguing because I want us to grow closer? (goodness)

To begin with, the initial move towards removing our ego and intense emotions from the disagreement is to recognize it. However, we must also understand that the desire to be right, the need to be superior, feeling offended, or wishing for a different reality do not actually resolve the problems at hand. In order to solve them collaboratively, we need to shift our attention towards the intention of enhancing the situation and reaching a more affectionate state. It may sound simple, but putting it into practice is far from easy. To achieve this, we must strive for a state of neutrality.

Notes/insights from the above:

_____

_____

_____

_____

_____

_____

TRY THIS: Identify Your Partner's Fight Style And Your Own
Check out the three styles listed below. Which one captures your personality the most accurately?

1. *Venting*. Some individuals, including myself, prefer to express their anger and continue discussing it until a resolution is reached. To put it differently, there are three perspectives in every argument: yours, mine, and the truth. There isn't an absolute truth. The fighter, who focuses on finding a solution, strives to reach an answer and often fixates excessively on facts. It's natural to have the desire to solve the problem, but if this resonates with you, it's important to remember to take a step back and create space not only for facts, which can be open to debate, but also for both sides of the story and the emotions of both you and your partner. Be cautious of unrestricted talking – in your eagerness to conclude things, you might overwhelm your partner with an excess of ideas and approaches. Avoid rushing towards a solution. First, you and your partner should come to an agreement on the issue at hand. Only then can you embark on seeking solutions together.

2. *Hiding*. In certain situations, some of us tend to shut down during an argument. The emotions become overwhelming, and they require some space to process everything. They may either become silent during the argument or leave the room to gather themselves before resuming the discussion. The person who withdraws does not wish to consider solutions in the midst of heightened emotions. They are not prepared to listen to them and might become even more irritated if their partner insists on a speedy resolution. It's important to take the necessary time and space, but it's crucial not to employ silence as a means of engaging in a conflict.

3. *Exploding*. There are those among us who struggle to contain their anger and end up bursting with intense emotions. This reaction significantly impacts our relationships, making it crucial to actively work on changing this behavior. If you find yourself in this category, it is important to focus on regulating your emotions. One approach could be seeking external assistance for anger management. Alternatively, you can collaborate with your partner during a calm period and establish a plan for the next disagreement, agreeing to take a time-out. Determine what method would be most effective for you, whether it's going for a jog, taking a refreshing shower, or finding other ways to release pent-up frustration.

To discover your personal fight style, check out the quiz at: www.FightStyles.com.

Notes/insights from the above:

_____

_____

_____

_____

_____

_____

_____

_____

_____

TRY THIS: Make An Agreement For Your Next Argument

It's simple to overlook our intentions when emotions are running high. However, if you have a prearranged and agreed-upon plan, you can rely on it during those heated moments. Here are a few key points to keep in mind. Take the time to discuss and agree on them with your partner during a peaceful moment. Then, when you find yourselves in the midst of an argument, pause for a moment. Use that count of ten to retrieve this agreement or access it on your phone.

CONFLICT AGREEMENT

Let's decide on a specific time and location to address this disagreement instead of dealing with it immediately.

We both acknowledge that reaching a mutual agreement leads to a win for both of us, whereas if one person wins, we both end up losing.

Our goal is to (choose any that apply): reach a compromise, empathize with each other's emotions, resolve this matter with a solution that prevents future arguments, support one another despite our differences.

A neutral description of the conflict that we agree on is:

_____

We're going to talk about it at this time:

_____

We're going to talk about it in this place:

_____

Prior to finding a solution, let's take a moment to individually jot down the reasons that are causing distress to the other person.

Here are four potential fixes to tackle the issue or approaches to prevent encountering this conflict in the future.

1.

_____

2.

_____

3.

_____

4.

_____

Are we both content with the outcome?

_____

TRY THIS: Discussing Complex Issues

We can't tackle intricate problems with simplistic agreements like "I'll make sure to always put my socks in the hamper" and "I'll remind you if you leave them on the floor." Significant issues may not have a simple solution or quick victory, and they demand deeper contemplation and effort to resolve. It all starts with expressing the problem clearly and engaging in joint contemplation. To help you get started and avoid the temptation to gloss over the problem with a superficial resolution, here are some approaches that will keep the matter open for further comprehension and discussion.

- "This is what I picked up on... And here's my plan for the future."
- "This particular aspect deeply resonated with me... and it has given me a fresh perspective."
- "Now I grasp your actual desires... Here's a practical way for me to respond."
- "I'm not entirely certain of the solution... but I genuinely care about you, and I'd appreciate revisiting this next week for further discussion."
- "I apologize for taking so long to really 'get' this. I now understand how it impacted you... Let's work together on resolving this."
- "I acknowledge the effort you're putting in... I'll be more patient and empathetic."

Recognize the insights you've gained about each other throughout this journey. When concluding this discussion, refrain from making promises that you cannot genuinely keep. Rather, focus on committing to what you will make an effort to do.

Notes/insights from the above:

_____

_____

_____

_____

_____

_____

_____

TRY THIS: Write An Apology Letter

Take a moment to ponder all the things you could say sorry to your partner for—every little thing that still lingers as a source of remorse. Remember, this exercise isn't about boosting your own ego or diminishing your self-worth. It's about acknowledging your errors, demonstrating accountability, and letting your partner know that you genuinely contemplate the impact you've had on them. It's a way to validate the emotions you might have overlooked, showing just how deeply you care.

For each mistake, list:

My mistake	
How it affected my partner	
Why I feel sorry	
How I will fix it or what I am going to do differently going forward	

My mistake	
How it affected my partner	
Why I feel sorry	
How I will fix it or what I am going to do differently going forward	

My mistake	
How it affected my partner	
Why I feel sorry	
How I will fix it or what I am going to do differently going forward	
My mistake	
How it affected my partner	
Why I feel sorry	
How I will fix it or what I am going to do differently going forward	

Avoid diluting your apology with blame, lengthy explanations, or excuses. The issue has already been discussed, and now your goal is to demonstrate your understanding of how you have hurt your partner. Once you have written your apology, hand it over to your partner. Make it clear that you have no expectations regarding their response; your intention is simply to express your love in a fresh manner by genuinely reflecting on past emotions, mistakes, or resentments that may have been left unaddressed or unresolved.

RULE 7: YOU DON'T BREAK IN A BREAKUP

TRY THIS: Check Your Reasons For Leaving

Are you genuinely pursuing this for your own sake, or have you been captivated by a flashy new individual? Take a moment to reflect and evaluate yourself.

CONSIDERATIONS

1. *Temptation check*. If the opportunity to meet the new person hadn't arisen, would you still choose to remain in your current relationship? If your answer is affirmative, then it would be wise to prioritize revitalizing the relationship.

2. *Reality check*. When a magician reveals the secrets behind a trick, its enchantment diminishes. Similarly, a new relationship is filled with magic, but it doesn't reveal what remains once the magic fades away. Keep in mind that even in a fresh relationship, cracks may eventually appear. Are you ready to address these issues as they arise, or will you find yourself trapped in the same cycle of frustration and disappointment?

3. *Karma check*. Keep in mind that if you leave for another person, there's a possibility that your new partner could do the same to you. It's crucial to ensure that if you choose to leave, it's because you sincerely believe that there is no future with your current partner and that you would prefer being by yourself rather than being with them.

Notes/insights from the above:

_____

_____

_____

_____

_____

_____

TRY THIS: Build A Support System

Find individuals who can provide assistance in important aspects of life. This is something you can do independently, but it's also an opportunity to involve your partner, allowing both of you to understand and be aware of each other's support networks.

Self. When you find yourself questioning your abilities, wantng to talk about your principles, exploring your spirituality, or wishing to commemorate your achievements, who do you seek for support?

_____

_____

Financial. Who would be the ideal person to offer guidance regarding your career, finances, and making financial choices? When it comes to mental and emotional well-being, which friends or sources can provide the necessary guidance and support for your mental health?

_____

_____

Health. Who can you approach when you have inquiries about your well-being? Who could be a reliable individual to seek support from when you face a challenging health concern, whether it's due to practical or emotional reasons?

_____

_____

Relationships. When you encounter difficulties or disagreements with friends, family, coworkers, or your significant other, who do you seek out for support and guidance?

_____

_____

Discovering your network of support jointly will enable you to recognize areas where you excel in supporting each other and identify opportunities to seek assistance from others without feeling guilty or ashamed from either perspective.

TRY THIS: Give Yourself Closure

Whether through voice notes or written form, express the pain inflicted by your partner. Share everything you wish to say to them about how they treated you and the impact it had on your emotions. This includes their words, actions, inquiries, accusations, traumatic incidents, and painful memories. Consider this compilation as an inventory of reasons why the breakup was ultimately for the best. If you've been fixating on the positive memories, it's essential to acknowledge the reality of the relationship.

So, document every challenge, mistake, and hurtful remark that deeply affected you. Is there anything your mind has been avoiding? Allow yourself to experience and process each emotion fully. Healing cannot take place until you truly feel. Simply walking away from something doesn't diminish its significance. Neglected emotions tend to intensify if not given the attention they deserve. To truly understand and acknowledge these emotions, articulate them, identify patterns, and provide explanations to yourself.

Next, alongside each action that caused you pain, identify who was responsible for it. Who performed the action? Who uttered hurtful words? Who engaged in actions that should never have been done? Sometimes, you may find that the responsibility lies with you. Recognizing this allows you to take ownership, make improvements, and foster personal growth.

You will also become conscious of the mistakes made by your ex-partner. There might have been negative aspects that you suppressed while you were in the relationship. We tend to do this because we subconsciously prefer familiar troubles. You knew they would be rude to you in the morning. You knew they would forget your birthday. You knew they would arrive late for dinner. You knew they would neglect to call or message you, despite your desire for it. You were aware of what they would get wrong, and it was easier to accept that than to face the uncertainty of being single, venturing into uncharted territory, not knowing how to feel, how to move forward, or what pain might arise next. We settle for less than we deserve in exchange for a sense of security. Familiar pain becomes our refuge.

Pain That My Partner Caused Me	Who Was Responsible For This? Who Took Action?

Pain That My Partner Caused Me	Who Was Responsible For This? Who Took Action?

By jotting down all the mishaps, you can shift your attention towards the positive aspects of this breakup. Search for a narrative that brings you closure. It's possible that you narrowly escaped a negative outcome. Perhaps you've learned a valuable lesson that you never want to experience again. Consider how this relationship could simply be a stepping stone on your journey towards healthier connections in the future.

Next, read aloud what you've written to an empty room. Although your ex won't be present to hear it, finding closure will come from the sense of sharing your thoughts and the understanding that you're crafting your own conclusion to aid in moving forward.

TRY THIS: Insights

Let's take a look at the recent history of your relationship to gather valuable insights that will help you in future relationships.

- Consider what you kept
- Consider what you let go
- Reflect on your own flaws
- Ask yourself: What have I discovered about myself through this relationship?

Get comfortable, put on something cozy, grab a warm drink, sit in front of a fireplace—choose a setting and approach that make you feel at ease and supported. This process may lead to some uncomfortable realizations, and that's alright. You might feel a mix of excitement and energy about certain aspects, while others might upset you. Remember, discomfort often accompanies the healing process.

Love has the power to obscure the faults and difficulties of others, while our desire to maintain a positive self-image can blind us to our own mistakes. When we are in love with someone, we tend to disregard their irritating or even harmful habits and behaviors. This activity aims to help us view those aspects with a fresh perspective.

Begin by questioning yourself: What aspects did I handle well in this relationship, and what do I wish to avoid repeating? Perhaps you often prioritized your own needs without truly listening to your partner. Alternatively, you might feel proud of establishing healthy boundaries, but your partner failed to respect them. Once again, take the time to jot it all down.

_____

_____

_____

_____

_____

Take a moment to ponder the benefits you derived from the relationship. Did you receive guidance, understanding, financial assistance, or support during challenging moments? Your partner undoubtedly brought value into your life at some point. Regardless of how much you believe you've lost or how painful the experience was, it's important to acknowledge and appreciate what they contributed to you.

_____

_____

_____

_____

_____

Now, take a moment to contemplate what you've sacrificed due to being in this relationship. Perhaps it's your sense of self-assurance that has wavered due to your partner's criticisms. Maybe you've lost precious time and energy. It's possible that you've missed out on connecting with other individuals or seizing opportunities because you were fully dedicated to this relationship.

_____

_____

_____

_____

_____

Last but not least, reflect on what went wrong in the relationship. What were the mistakes you committed? Did the relationship test your ability to remain authentic to yourself? Did it challenge your notions of what constitutes a desirable partner? It's crucial to pose these tough questions to yourself and find honest answers. Failing to address and learn from the mistakes they uncover will only result in repeating them with another person.

_____

_____

_____

_____

TRY THIS: Checklist To See If You're Ready To Date Again

☐ Did I absorb the valuable insights from my previous relationship that will pave the way for a more fulfilling partnership in the future?

_____

_____

☐ What should I keep in mind?

_____

_____

☐ What do I aim to steer clear of?

_____

_____

☐ What are the key things I want my future partner to know about me from the beginning?

_____

_____

☐ Do I have a clear understanding of my values and aspirations in this phase of my life? If not, I can dedicate some alone time to reevaluate these aspects.

_____

_____

☐ Do I have a clear understanding of the limits I wish to establish for my future partner? I might be interested in entering the dating scene again, but I want to ensure that I take things slow and not rush into anything.

_____

_____

☐ Am I interested in establishing boundaries when it comes to physical interactions?

_____

_____

☐ Should I delay becoming exclusive?

_____

_____

☐ Should I make sure not to bail on any plans like I did before, for someone similar to the previous incident?

_____

_____

Lastly, if you're uncertain about your readiness to enter the dating scene again, give it a shot. There's no need to make it an official dating or non-dating situation. Just gauge how it makes you feel.

Part Four: Connection: Learning To Love Everyone

RULE 8: LOVE AGAIN AND AGAIN

TRY THIS: Help A difficult Family Member Find Love In Their Community

If you find it challenging to express love directly to a close friend or family member, you can still encompass them within your circle of love by assisting them in discovering other sources of affection. Help them find new companions. Introduce them to individuals who share similar interests. Inquire with your friends if they know anyone in the same area who might connect well with this person.

Discover services that can benefit them. Connect them with a spiritual community, local fitness center, or arrange for assistance with tasks they struggle with or dislike doing.

Support them in pursuing their passions. For instance, you can assist a lonely parent in starting a book club or organizing a poker tournament.

Organize a family gathering in a neutral location. Being in a public setting tends to alleviate tensions and improve everyone's behavior. If visiting each other's homes feels too overwhelming, consider meeting at a restaurant or another public place where both of you feel comfortable.

Send them a heartfelt appreciation letter. Express your cherished moments together, convey your admiration for them, and acknowledge the positive impact they have had on your life.

Actions, notes and insights from the above:

_____

_____

_____

_____

_____

TRY THIS: Structure Your List Of Loved Ones

Create a roster of your extended network of friends and family. (Using your social media friend or follower lists can be a starting point. Facebook and Instagram provide options to categorize friends based on the level of online information they receive.)

Now, do the same exercise in real-life interactions. Classify this list into categories such as close friends and family, good friends and family, significant contacts, and acquaintances.

Determine how much time you can allocate to each category. For instance, you might decide to connect or make plans with close friends and family on a weekly basis, and good friends once a month. Alternatively, you may choose to reach out to meaningful contacts every quarter and acquaintances once a year.

This breakdown helps you be mindful of how you want to distribute your time and allows you to convey this to your network. For instance, you can say, "I'd love to have lunch together once a month." While it may seem unusual to inform your significant contacts that you've assigned them a quarterly frequency, having it in mind that you catch up with them every season, perhaps during holidays, helps you stay in touch and stay aware of their life events.

If you struggle to form friendships or have recently relocated and are starting anew, this compilation can serve as a reminder of the individuals you hold dear. Are there relatives or casual acquaintances whom you desire to develop closer bonds with? Keeping a dynamic list of those who intrigue you and whom you genuinely care about will assist you in establishing a supportive circle.

Name	Category	Time To Connect
Name 1	Close friend and family	Once a week
Name 2	Good friend and family	Once a month
Name 3	Meaningful contact	Once every quarter
Name 4	Acquaintance	Twice a year

Name	Category	Time To Connect

TRY THIS: Bring Love To Work

1. *Understanding.* You don't have to delve into their deepest desires and understand them as intimately as you would with your closest friends and family. However, show interest in their personal lives and make an effort to keep up with their ups and downs, especially when they have valid reasons to be preoccupied and require extra support from you. Be attentive to any shifts in your colleagues' moods and follow up on the challenges you know they're facing. If they're going through a difficult phase, consider if there's a way you can assist them by taking on additional tasks or finding ways to ease their burden.

Acknowledge the effort they put into their work, recognize their accomplishments, and take note of their progress. Celebrate their successes.

2. *Connection.* Whether you're connecting online or in real life, kick off your day or a meeting by touching base with your coworker. Take a moment to gauge how their day is unfolding. Show interest in the personal matters they've previously discussed with you. Make it a more humanized experience rather than immediately delving into the agenda.

3. *Appreciation.* Each day, select a colleague from your work life to send a short message, whether through a voicemail, text, or email, expressing appreciation or gratitude for something specific they have done at work.

Engage in these gestures with the intention of spreading more love in the world, without anticipating or demanding any reciprocation from your coworkers.

Notes/insights from the above:

_____

_____

_____

_____

_____

_____

You made it to the end!

Thank you.

Thank you so much for picking up the Workbook for Jay Shetty's *8 Rules of Love*. We really hope you enjoyed it, and that it helped you practise the lessons in everyday life.

If you'd like to give feedback on the book, or to find more workbooks for other self-development books, join us at BigActionBooks.com.

Thanks again,
The Big Action Books team

BigActionBooks.com

Made in the USA
Las Vegas, NV
24 October 2023

79557442R10046